Certificate:

FOLIO 03-2020-021011274700-01
INDAUTOR
First edition, 2018
Email: cpcarlosramos@cprqconsultoria.com
Web: www.cprqconsultoria.com

Editorial Design:
Enter Creativos
www.entercreativos.com /
hola@entercreativos.com

ORIENTATION TO ACCOUNTING FOR NON-ACCOUNTANTS

BY CARLOS RAMOS

This book talks about the personal experience of a CPA Specialized in Finance of what Accounting is and how it is used in companies to analyze information in a way that helps to generate more profits.

All businesses owners, administrators and key personnel need to know the numbers (Accounting) in a basic way, to be able to get the business on the right track and get maximum benefits from it. This book explains what Accounting is in a simple way, without CPA's technical words, with clear explanations and practical examples so that everyone who wants to learn Accounting, can do it.

In this book you will find the basic information necessary to start understanding the finances of your business, you will understand the numbers and how you can use Accounting in small and medium businesses to analyze the information in a way that helps to get more profits.

This book explains step-by-step, with simple examples, how Reports (Financial Statements) and business analysis are made and how they can help us in decision making.

This book also talks about the benefits of being a business owner and how to seek financial freedom.

SALTILLO, COAHUILA

DEDICATION

To my son Carlos, of 17 years old, since this book started as a writing for him because it caught my attention that he told me that one of the options he was considering for his career was to be a CPA.

I liked that he wanted to do something where I can teach him and guide him more easily than in other careers that I do not know the technical details of them, even if I may know most of the activities they do.

But the most important thing is that he can do something that he likes, something that he enjoys doing and that's why I decided to structure in an understandable way for him, an explanation of what an Accountant does, so that he had more clear understanding of the activities that he would be doing if he choose this career and be sure that it is something that he likes.

While I was writing this book, I realized that this kind of explanation could be pretty helpful to me if I had heard it before I started studying, because even when I ended the Career as CPA, it was not clear for me the different activities that I could do.

The words that I use in this book, are the ones that I can use to explain in a better way to someone who has no knowledge of accounting (as my son), so the meaning of some words will not be the same as the ones used in Wikipedia or by the CPA Institutions.

ACKNOWLEDGMENTS

To my parents, Dr. Carlos Ramos and Dr. Lupita Quiñones, who are the two persons that I most admire. Thank you for educated me with your example and values, that made it easier for me to relate with extraordinary people.

To my wife Diana for supporting me, take care of me, understand me and for being (together with my children Carlos, Mariana and Patricio) what I love the most and the reason why I always seek to improve myself.

To my Grandma María, because she is the one who prays the most for me. Although I had to teach her how to pray, because she only asked "work" for me ... and there I was working late until Saturdays and Sundays. I already told her to ask for Health, Love and Money, I'll take care of work.

To my sisters, aunts, uncles, cousins and all my relatives that always support me.

To my friends and compadres … they are few, but they are enough because they are excellent people.

CONTENTS

I.- HOW TO UNDERSTAND BETTER

Something that has worked in me to understand things, is to go from the global to the specific and not from the specific to the global, as is generally done in all schools and universities.

Usually they start teaching math, algebra, physics, accounting, etc. We attend classes, we pay attention and we do the homework, but we don't know how we are going to use that in real life.

It reminds me at the Karate Kid movie (the original with Daniel San and Mr. Miyagi).

In this film, Mr. Miyagi (the teacher) told Daniel San (a karate beginner) "wax-on, wax-off", so that he could wax cars all day long and Daniel San did it, although he didn't liked it, just because someone who knows Karate was telling him, but he didn't know how that would be helpful in a fight.

At the end Daniel San wants to give up because he is tired of doing all the nonsense things ordered by Mr. Miyagi, in that moment the great master arrives and explains Daniel Sam through a fight against him, that the repetitive movements that were made when waxing cars, painting fences, sanding floors, etc., were a specific training in important areas so that these movements together, will be pretty helpful at a fight.

Something similar happens at school, the subjects are those important areas that we must have for the fight and this is very good, however in the majority of the schools (if not in all of them - at least none of the schools a where I studied) the great master doesn't appear at the end and we leave school without knowing how all that we learned will help us.

There is a graduation ceremony where you get a diploma, in which your relatives go, they all congratulate you and tell you that you are ready ... but ready to do what?

I see it as if we want to explain the planet earth to someone who doesn't know it and we begin telling him about the rivers, mountains, flora, fauna, etc. I think it would be easier to explain it first with the world map and then the details of rivers, etc.

I was taught at the beginning with classes in Accounting, Tax, Costs, International Business, etc. And I had excellent teachers, but even when I finish College, I was not clear about all the activities that a CPA could do.

II.- WHAT IS ACCOUNTING AND WHAT IS A COMPANY?

𝕿he first thing that should be clear is what accounting is and what a company is.

What is accounting?

Accounting is a way of putting all the information related to the economic operations of a person or a company so that it can give us a picture (with numbers) of the situation of the Company. That picture should tell us the size of the company, level of sales and costs, what profits or losses are generated each month, as well as what is owned, what is owed and how they were generated.

What is a company? There are many kinds of companies, but it is usually a place where several people (including an accountant) meet for a common purpose.

Who makes a company? Companies are made by a person or a group of people (owner or owners) who put resources, which in many cases is money. This part is very important, since every business requires an investment and many times a second or third investment before it starts to generate profits. Owners should be aware of this and should be ready to do it if necessary.

How is a company made? The owners of the company review product information, such as market acceptance, competition, financial projections, etc. and if they see that the business is going to have profits, they proceed to make the company.

What is a company made for? The company is made with a purpose, which is the Mission and besides of generating profits (with the exception of non-profit companies such as Charity), it must seek to do something for society, at least for a small group of people that is the possible customers that the business can reach.

As an example, the Google Mission is "to organize the world's information and make it universally accessible and useful". Obviously the company generates big profits, but it is important that all managers and employees at all levels know and feel committed to the Mission of the company.

Besides of the Mission, companies have a Vision, which is where they see themselves in the future.

It is important that all personnel know where the company is targeting, so that everyone collaborates on it.

And for this reason, the values of the company must be established, for example if the vision is to reach 100,000 products sold per year ... it should not be fooling customers with bad products, although some companies do this, they do not remain a long time in business.

Some companies use values such as honesty, excellence, humility, etc. as a basis to achieve their vision.

It is very important that companies have a mission, vision and values that guide each of its members in their actions, although many companies do not have them in writing and most of them do not communicate them adequately to all people or do not follow them.

How do you start a company? We must have a legal consultant, there are companies that have an entire area with several lawyers, although this is not essential, but at least we must have the legal advice of a lawyer. This person is very important, not only for the start of the company, but for the operation of the business.

A kind of company is chosen and a series of processes are needed to make the company, such as requesting the name, making the charter, applying for Social Security ID, Tax ID, etc. That each of these processes takes several days or weeks, there are countries that do it faster and others that do it slower.

Who does what? There is an Organization Chart with activities for each position, where the structure is established by the owners or administrators.

Human resources (people) must be aligned with the objectives of the company, the activities must be divided among the members in an equitable manner, the workloads for each member must be balanced and the salaries must be fair.

Who runs a company? The structure depends on the size and needs of each company, but generally it is a General Manager, who reports the results to the owners of the company. The Production Manager, the Sales Manager and the Controller reports to the General Manager and the rest of the employees report to them.

Although from my point of view the Controller must be independent of the General Manager, he should report directly to the owners and be the one who presents the monthly results with them.

So what we understand as company:

As we mentioned above, there are many kinds of companies, but it is generally a place where several people (including an accountant) meet for a common purpose, which is the mission of the company and who work together to achieve the business objectives.

This applies to all kinds of companies, large, medium and small. Although in real life many businesses don't do it (they don't have a mission, they don't have advise from a lawyer, they are not prepared for a second investment, they don't have accounting analysis, etc.), but also in real life many businesses do not last longer than one year.

ACTIVITIES THAT ARE DONE IN THE COMPANY

Once the Owners gave the resources (money) to the company, that we have the Mission, the we have the activities that each one is going to do and the product that is going to be sold, the next thing to do is Produce and Sell.

These two activities (Produce - Sell) are easy to say, but depending on the kind of company, these activities have several processes and sub processes that make them difficult to perform and analyze.

As an example I'm going to use an imaginary company that produces engines for cars. I want to use a large company as an example, since the processes are more complicated and if the process of the large company is understood, it will be easier to understand the ones of a small company.

This company seeks to sell engines for cars, but for this purpose, first you have to buy materials such as steel (or scrap to have a lower cost), other metals and chemicals that are the raw material to make the engines.

Then you have to melt them and for this it is necessary to have people to do it, as well as add additional materials in the process.

You should also make a mold (which involves buying other materials such as graphite) to cool the melted metals and give it the shape of the engine.

After that, we need to check that the product meets the necessary quality (that is not broken, that has the form and appropriate measures, etc).

Finally the product is packed and sold to the customer (which implies transportation).

With the activities mentioned above we cover in an easy way the complete process to produce and sell the product.

III.- WHICH ACTIVITIES PEOPLE DO IN THE PROCESS ?

$\mathfrak{N}$ow let's see what activities people do in order to make the process that we saw:

A. Initially one or several people make the purchase of materials (such as scrap, chemicals and graphite), they request quotes from different suppliers to get the best price, quality, delivery time, etc. to finally make the purchase.

B. There are people from the company who receive the materials physically from the suppliers, they stamp the supplier's invoice and they entered the invoice into the system so it can appear available for later registration by accounting.

C. There are people in accounting who review the supplier's documentation and receive the material in the system.

D. Once registered by Accounting, the material appears available for use and production personnel, in this example from the Melting area, pick up the material (scrap and chemicals) from the warehouse and then melts it.

E. At the same time, Molds personnel pick up the graphite from the warehouse and makes the mold to have it ready and as soon as the steel is melted, it is placed in the mold so that it cools and takes the shape of the engine.

F. Once the engine is cold, it is taken out of the mold and checked by quality personnel, who indicate whether the product can be packaged or rejected.

G. Once accepted by the Quality staff, the personnel of the Packaging area proceeds to pack it and have it available for sale.

H. It is then sold to the Customer and physically delivered, which means carrying it in a truck (dry boxes, as those trucks are called). To do it you must make the invoice with the necessary documentation to take the product out of the company.

So far we already know what is the process of a large company and the activities that people do on it.

Small companies do (or they should do) the same activities, but many times all the activities are done by one or two persons.

IV.- WHICH ACTIVITIES ARE DONE BY ACCOUNTANTS?

Not all the activities we saw are done by Accountants, there are activities that are made by the Purchasing area (which are generally not accountants), others by the Logistics area (which are generally Engineers), others by the productive areas (which are generally Engineers), etc.

This book is focused only on the activities that Accountants do in the company, because we are analyzing Accounting and how it can help to increase profits.

Now we will see the activities and we will relate each activity to the example that we are seeing of the motor company and we will identify it with the sign "++".

Before we continue with the example, I want to mention that there are two kinds of approaches for Accounting; the Fiscal approach and the Financial approach.

Many companies use the Fiscal approach, this approach seeks to comply with fiscal obligations (pay taxes) and in this approach an accountant specialized in Taxes is required to do the tax strategy and the calculations for presentation to the IRS and pay the less possible amount of taxes, because taxes could be one of the biggest expenses for the companies. This Accountant must be specialized in taxes.

The Financial approach seeks to generate useful information for analysis and decision making. This requires more detail in the information and longer time of the Accountant to perform the analysis properly, sometimes even requires some investment in software to perform the analysis mentioned. This requires a specialized accountant in Finance and depending on the kind of industry and size of the company, several accountants are required to do it properly and with excellence.

Accounting

---> Fiscal Approach; lower cost for the company. And lower payment of taxes.

---> Financial Approach; higher cost, but the benefit of better analysis for decision making is bigger.

It is important to remember that we are looking at a large company that requires a Financial approach, in which a good analysis is needed.

Not only large companies require the financial approach, now more and more businesses are looking for good analysis that will help them to have better control of the company and increase profits.

Well, we have already seen that many companies look for the Fiscal approach and this approach is indispensable either if you have the financial approach or not. For the Fiscal approach an Accountant specialized in Taxes is needed as well as the correct registration of all the records (transactions) which implies (based on the size of the company) to have several accountants to pay, register the records, etc. However this approach doesn't need cost analysis, financial analysis and other activities that we'll see in the Financial approach.

Now we'll look at the Financial approach and we'll continue with the example of the big company that makes engines. Accountants are in the Finance area and although the activities vary from company to company, they are generally the following nine for the Financial approach:

1.- Accounts Receivable; in this area the invoices from customers are recorded (reviewing that the sales documentation as invoice, remission, packing slip, etc., is correct). ++ In the example we are looking at, the shipping staff will deliver the documents as the invoice so that the Accountant can make the invoice properly.

Reports of income and credit sales are made in this area, as well as aging analysis, with this reports actions are taken to reduce the accounts receivable to the minimum (have the less possible money owed, in order to have the money available to buy more material or invest it in a project).

2.- Acounts Payable; This area records the invoices of all suppliers, ++ in this example the scrap suppliers. The documentation delivered by the suppliers is reviewed (such as supplier invoice, receipt stamps, purchase order, bill of lading, etc) to make the records.

Reports for analysis by supplier and by aging are made in this area in order to keep track of the suppliers and analyze metrics comparing what we owe to suppliers vs what customers owes us, that will help us to make decisions in order to have a better cash flow for our business.

3.- Payroll; In this area the payroll is made, the incidents (absenteeism, etc.) are reviewed and taxes and social security obligations are considered. The weekly, biweekly or monthly payroll is registered and controlled with reports for analysis by areas and concepts (number of people - head count, overtime, holidays, etc).

++ In the example that we are looking at, the supervisors of each area (materials, melting, molds, packaging, etc.) send to the Payroll Accountant the absenteeism and delays of each one of their employees. The Payroll Accountant makes the calculations based on the respective salaries and taxes and makes the payroll receipts complying with the tax requirements.

These three areas (Accounts Receivable, Accounts Payable and Payroll) of Finance have to do with the productive process that we mentioned above, since they make the invoices to customers, record invoices of suppliers and make the payroll.

However there are other activities that accountants do that are not directly related to the production process, but are necessary to control and analyze the business, which are the following six areas:

4.- Taxes; calculation and presentation of local, state and federal taxes. ++ That in this example are mainly the taxes from engines sales, but there are other taxes such as those mentioned in the previous point of payroll. There are also taxes such as VAT.

5.- Accounting; in this area the financial operations of the company are recorded, although most of the records are made by the system, those records are reviewed so they have been made in the correct accounts. ++ In the example of the engines, we will review how each of the 8 activities that people do (from A to H, which we saw in Content III) are registered.

"A" Purchases and "B" Receipt of materials, are not recorded in accounting, it is required to keep track of them, but we can have internal reports or controls that don't generate a record in accounting.

"C" Invoice Registration, when the supplier's invoice is recorded, the system makes the register according to the data provided in the record. The Accounting area checks that it has been made in the correct accounts. And for raw materials, the Costs area is the one that makes the review.

"D" y "E" Material Delivery to production, is recorded by the system at the moment in which the warehouse personnel register the delivery of the material to production personnel. The Accounting area checks that the records have been made in the correct accounts.

"F" Quality review is not recorded in accounting, but it is required to keep track of this with an internal report or control separately.

"G" The packaging is recorded, it is not reviewed by the Accounting area, but by the Costs area, since this has to do directly with the cost of the product.

"H" Sale and delivery to the Client, the personnel of shipments registers the data so that personnel of Finances can make the billing, making sure to comply with tax requirements. The invoice is recorded by the system and the Accounting area review that the records have been made in the correct accounts.

Besides these eight activities (which, as we have just mentioned, some are recorded in Accounting and others are not), there are closing records (such as depreciation, interest, insurance amortization, etc.) that are made in this area to complete the accounting.

Weekly and monthly reports are also made to compare the income vs expenses and analyze the profit of the company.

6.- Costs; in this area the cost per unit is calculated (the cost per piece), since in that way analysis of the break even point can be made (which is the quantity of products that the company must sell in order not to lose), as well as gross profit, volume and price variations, analysis by products or processes and other analyzes that are useful for decision making.

In this area, the cost review of the areas discussed in previous points is made, as well as inventory valuation and control.

7.- Financial Analyst; analysis of the different accounts that were strategically created in order to see which ones require more attention, in general this area provides information to the administration in order to evaluate the efficiency of the operation of the company.

8.- Internal Auditor; review that the records made by the other accountants are correct, it is always good to have a validation.

9.- Controller; leads the other accountants and is responsible for analyzing and presenting the information with the Administration for decision making.

Depending on the size and needs of the company, each of the areas (except Controller) can have several Accountants. In small companies all activities are made by one person, but they need to make sure is that all activities are done, because all of them are necessary good information that can help us to make the reports to analyze the business and make decisions.

In general these nine are the activities that Accountants do in companies.

An important thing to say is that in the area of Finance all the information is Confidential, so if you want to be an Accountant, this is something you will always live with ... you should tattooed "confidentiality". The information is not yours, it belongs to the company and you must protect it, so that only the owners or administrators of the company can see it. The Financial Statements, payments, sales, etc., you must take care of everything so that others do not see it and you have to take special care in the payroll, since there is a lot of curiosity in people wanting to know the salaries of other people.

WHAT ARE THE EXTERNAL ACCOUNTANTS AND WHAT DO THEY DO?

The External Accountants are usually Accounting Firms that specialize in the different areas of Accounting and that have personnel to make the activities for several companies.

External accountants do the same activities as the company's accountants. Companies choose between both options depending on the level of experience that is required and the cost-benefit that they will obtain.

All the activities or some of them can be subcontracted to an Accounting Firm. It is common to see companies that outsource the Audit and Taxes, there are other companies that also outsource the payroll and financial analysis and there are others that outsource all the services of the Finance area.

I have worked in companies that have more than 20 Accountants in the different Finance areas and also be in companies that outsource most of the activities. I could not say that any of these options is better for all companies, since it depends on the activities that the business seeks and the level of experience required for it.

V.- HOW THE RECORDING IN ACCOUNTING IS MADE?

The way to do it is the "double-entry", which means that everything we do has two actions.

It is very important that we can understand this very well, because this will help us understand other accounting subjects. It 's normal that we don't get it at the first time, so you can read this topic several times until everything is clear.

Before starting to make the records, the company defines the accounts that are going to be used as Banks, Accounts Receivable, Inventories, Accounts Payable, Equity, etc. The number of accounts and the detail in them depends on the analysis needed by each company.

We are going to make an example of the accounting of a company with only 3 records (transactions) and we are going to assume that it is a trading company that buys computer monitors in China online and sells the same product in Mexico.

Record 1. When we start the company we receive money from the owner and as we mentioned "Everything" has two actions that we will call A and B:

A.- One action is that we have money in the bank.

B.- And the other action is that there is a shareholder (equity increase).

Record 2. After we received the money, we make the first purchase of materials with that money that the owner (shareholder) invested:

A.- One action is that we have material in our company (or warehouse) to use it later to produce and sell.

B.- And the other action is that we reduce the bank's money, because we make the payment to the supplier.

Record 3. The product is sold in Mexico:

A.- One action is that we have more money in the bank for the payment from the Client.

B.- Another that we made a sale.

A.- When selling you also have a cost of selling (of the product sold).

B.- And you have less material in the warehouse because a product was sold.

As we can see in record 3, there were four actions. There are records that will have more than two actions, especially when we register taxes, but for this example we will leave it in this way (without taxes) to make it easier.

These actions (A and B) are called debits and credits and what you have to do is identify which action is debit and which one is credit. The name can be the one you like, it can be A and B, debits and credits, pears and apples, whatever you want to call them but it should always be the same amount in the debits as in the credits, this is what the accountants call " a balance ".

The accountants put this in a diagram so they can see it better and they call it "T" accounts because that's the shape of the diagram.

Let's put numbers to the example ... Let's say those 3 were the only records of the month and we will not consider taxes for this practical example.

1. The shareholder put $ 500 dollars.
2. We buy 3 monitors in China each one for $ 150 dollars (total $ 450).
3. And we sell two monitors with one month credit at $ 200 dollars each (total $ 400).

We create the following accounts that the company will use:

Banks, Owner's Investment, Inventory, Accounts Receivable, Sales and Cost of Sales.
The accounting records are the following:

M1 Shareholder contribution of $500

Action	Account	Debit		Credit	
A	Banks	$	500		
B	Owner's Investment			$	500

M2 Purchase of 3 monitors at $150 each

Action	Account	Debit		Credit	
A	Inventory	$	450		
B	Banks			$	450

M3 Credit Sales of 2 monitors at $400

Action	Account	Debit		Credit	
A	Accounts receivable	$	400		
B	Sales			$	400
A	Cost of sales	$	300		
B	Inventory			$	300

The T accounts will be as follows (the M1, M2 and M3 are included next to each movement):

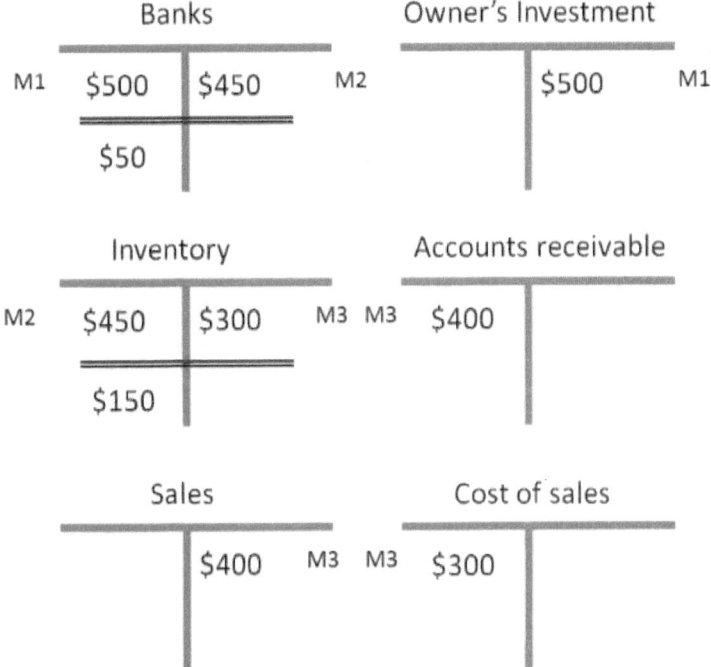

As we can see, in the Banks account and the Inventories account there were two records, if there are several records, those that are on the left in the "T" account are subtracted from the ones on the right and the difference is placed in the side of which is greater. In the case of Banks we had $ 500 on the left side from Record one and $ 450 on the right side from Record two, so the difference of $ 50 is on the left side.

These calculations will help us later to make the Reports that we'll use to analyze our business.

VI.- REPORTS (FINANCIAL STATEMENTS)

It's very important that we can analyze the numbers of our business, the ones who doesn't to it, are not going to be able to get the maximum benefit from the business and probably they will put it in risk, because in order to make decisions, we need to have a clear picture of the business and without correct reports, this can't be done.

We use the records to make the Reports, the accounting systems do this automatically, but if it's not a big company or does not have too many records, we can keep the accounting in Excel, the only thing we should look for, is to have as much detail as possible to be able to make the analysis of costs by unit. The Reports can be done with pivot tables (which is a tool that is easy to use in Excel).

The Reports or Financial Statements most used by Companies are the Income Statement, Balance Sheet and Cash Flow.

The Income Statement or Profit and Loss (P&L), shows the results, profit or loss that the company had in a period of time, which is normally a month, but can be analyzed bimonthly, semester, year, etc.

An easy way to show it is the following:

Sales
- Cost of Sales
= Gross Profit
- Operating Expenses
= Operating Profit
- Financial Expenses
= Profit before taxes
- Taxes
= Net Profit

But usually in companies each one of these accounts have subaccounts, to get a more detailed analysis based in the business needs.

The Balance Sheet shows the economic and financial situation of a company at a certain date. This financial statement is cumulative, unlike the Income Statement that is made per month. For example, if we look at the Reports for the month of June, the Income Statement is the profit or loss of June and the Balance Sheet is the accumulated amount until the month of June.

It has three main areas, the Assets is what the company has. The Liability is what the company owes and the Equity is the contribution of the shareholders plus the accumulated profits of the company.

ASSETS	LIABILITIES + EQUITY
	LIABILITIES
Current Assets	**Current Liabilities**
Banks	Suppliers
Accounts Receivable	Other accounts payable
Inventories	**Total Current Liabilities**
Total Current Assets	**Long term liabilities**
	Lomg Term Debt
Fixed Assets	**Total Long term liabilities**
Fixed Assets	**Total Liabilities**
Accumulated Depreciation	**Equity**
Total Fixed Assets	Owner's Investment
	Retained earnings
	Total Equity
TOTAL ASSETS	**TOTAL LIABILITIES + EQUITY**

Capital = Assets - Liabilities

Or in other words:

The company is = What the company have - What the company owes.

In this example, considering that there were only those three records and that we do not have taxes, the Income Statement will look like this:

	USD	
Sales	$	400
- Cost of Sales	$	300
= Gross Profit	$	100
- Operating Expenses	$	-
= Operating Profit	$	100
- Financial Expenses	$	-
= Profit before taxes	$	100
- Taxes	$	-
= Net Profit	$	100	A

We took the amounts of this report from the calculations that we made in the "T" accounts:

The sales and the cost of sales are those related to the two monitors and from those accounts the Gross Profit is generated, which is a profit that is not Final since other expenses need to be considered.

In this example we do not have Operating Expenses, but in real life there are payroll, rent, utilities, services, etc. We also didn't include Financial Expenses, which are mainly related to loan interest. We didn't include in the example taxes either, but are the ones mentioned above that are mainly due to profits that the business has.

And subtracting all these expenses, we get the Net Profit or Final Profit, which is the gain of the business.

This information is used by the owners and managers of the company for analysis, obviously there are more records and more accounts, so it is important to define the accounts that we want to analyze, because based on these analyzes, the decisions are made, like how to increase or reduce prices, look for better costs in areas of higher consumption, reduce accounts receivable, eliminate a product when it is not profitable or increase it when it is very profitable, etc.

In this example we can see in the Income Statement that the profit that we had by selling two products was $100 dollars. You have to see what fixed expenses the business would have, such as payroll, electricity, gas, water, rent, etc. to be able to make analyzes like the break even point, where you calculate how many products you have to sell so that the business does not lose money. This kind of information is important to know, because based on this, objectives are set in the company.

The Balance Sheet in this example would look like this:

ASSETS			LIABILITIES + EQUITY			
			LIABILITIES			
Current Assets			**Current Liabilities**			
Banks	$	50	Suppliers	$	-	
Accounts Receivable	$	400	Other accounts payable	$	-	
Inventories	$	150	**Total Current Liabilities**	$	-	
Total Current Assets	$	600	**Long term liabilities**			
			Lomg Term Debt	$	-	
Fixed Assets			**Total Long term liabilities**	$	-	
Fixed Assets	$	-	**Total Liabilities**	$	-	
Accumulated Depreciation	$	-	**Equity**			
Total Fixed Assets	$	-	Owner's Investment	$	500	
			Retained earnings	$	100	A
			Total Equity	$	600	
TOTAL ASSETS	$	600	**TOTAL LIABILITIES + EQUITY**	$	600	

The information for this report is also taken from the "T" accounts and we can see that in Banks are the $ 50 that we calculate. In the example we did not put Fixed Assets (Building, Machinery, etc), nor that we have debts with suppliers, nor banks.

In this Financial Statement, the Total Assets must be equal to the amount of Liability + Equity, which in this example is $ 600 dollars.

As we can see (with the letter A both in the graph of the Income Statement and in the one of the

Balance Sheet) the profit of the Income Statement is transferred to the Balance Sheet in the accumulated profits account. And in that line is where we summarize the profits or losses accumulated until a certain month.

On the other hand, the Balance Sheet tells us that we have accounts receivable of $400 and that we only have $50 in Bank, so one of our activities must be to collect those $400 so that they become money available to buy more products.

In real companies there are more accounts in the Income Statement and more accounts in the General Balance (sometimes even by client or supplier), which are created by the owners or administrators to be able to make analyzes that allow them to make actions such as the ones we mentioned previously.

The Cash Flow in this example will look like this:

Cash flow from operative activities	-$	450
+/- Cash flow from investment activities	$	500
+/- Cash flow from financing activities	$	-
= Cash Flow of the period	$	50
+ Bank Begining Balance	$	-
= Bank Ending Balance	$	50

This report shows us the details of the bank account and must match the $ 50 dollars that we have in Banks in the Balance Sheet Report.

We can see in this report that we have $ 50 dollars in the Bank account, but the operation cash flow is negative because the sale was on credit and in the month we didn't receive money from the operation, so we must make actions to collect that money and change the operation cash flow to positive.

In real companies there are more accounts in the Income Statement, more accounts in the Balance Sheet (sometimes even by customer or supplier) and more detail in the Cash Flow, which are created by the owners or administrators, in order to make analysis that allow them to make actions like those mentioned above.

In this book we will not see those details since the intention is that we understand the way that accounting can helps us to analyze our business and make decisions to increase our profit.

VII.- BE THE OWNER OF YOUR BUSINESS

What I mean is that the business owners are the ones who can manage it with very few hours of their time or only with monthly reviews.

And not the ones that operate the business as self-employed, which in many times are underpaid.

We must analyze this point when we put our business, since many times the profits we get are lower than the salary that we can get if we worked in a company or for someone else, besides the fact that we spend more time and all the responsibility lies with us.

I am not saying that being an employee is better than a business owner, I think it is the opposite, since as a business owner you can have financial freedom, more time available for family, friends, sports, etc. However, there are many businesses in which the owners work as self-employed and do not achieve financial freedom, nor have more time for the family, etc.

And this is mainly because they don't analyze the business with the reports we mentioned above and therefore don't know the numbers of their business and don't make actions to make it grow and take it to the next level.

This next level consists in being able to systematize the business, that means, to have the procedures of each process (including both the productive one and the administrative one from sales, purchases, records, inventories, fixed assets, organization chart, human resources, hiring, levels of authorization, etc.), as well as the necessary team so that the business can operate without the owner being present.

It's necessary to hire the right people for each position of the business and this is where it becomes complicated because many times the Owners don't want to delegate the production activities they do because they think that nobody can do it better than them and it gets more complicated when they need to hire a general manager to operate the business. But this are necessary steps to really be the business owner and to be able to achieve the financial and time freedom you are looking for.

Both being able to analyze the numbers, as well as doing the procedures to systematize the business, are not easy to do for most business owners, because they are very good at operating, but nobody taught them administration and many times it is necessary for them to have the advice of a business coach, who are people with experience in these issues that can guide them to achieve it.

VIII.- OTHER ADVICES

I worked in important positions of large companies (Finance Director, Controller, Accounting Manager, etc.) and I am proud to say that I was not fired from any company, I went out of the companies in good way and the exit was due to better job offers.

I worked 4 years average in each company and I want to tell you how I managed to stay in good positions for so many years in all the companies in which I worked for.

It is not because I was the most prepared, nor the most intelligent. I consider myself intelligent and I studied in a good schools (ITESM Campus Monterrey), I have a Master's Degree in Finance from the same school and I speak two languages, but I know that there is always someone more prepared and more smart than you.

I achieved the positions I had for the Trust that people had in me and for the ability to make relations, based on respect, with all people.

As you advance in the levels of the company, you will realize that each time the technical part is less important and the administrative part (communication, leadership, etc.), becomes more important.

When you work as an Accountant, you have make records, run processes, etc. However, when you work as a Controller or Finance Director, the job is to guide (lead) people from the Finance area as well as from other areas and even people outside the company (suppliers, banks, Treasury, Government, etc.) and there is more relationships and supervision activities than doing things.

I would like to give you a lot of advices, but I think the main ones are the following:

+ Get closer to God (whatever your religion is) and thank him for what you have, we all have a gift, we must use it to help others. Everything God does is for a reason and even when we do not understand it, we must know that it has a purpose.

+ Enjoy life, live the present, this word means gift ... the gift that God gives you.

Enjoying is synonymous of helping. This may sound weird, but really when you help someone you enjoy more. The businesses with Mission's on helping customers, employees, suppliers, enjoy the work more and they are more successful because of it.

+ Be humble, the word humility comes from the word humus, which means dust and what it means is that we are all dust and on dust we will become or in other words we are all equal, it doesn't matter if the person is rich or poor and neither If it is of another nationality or race, we must treat everyone as equals.

Humility is not synonymous of poverty, it is synonymous of quality of person.

+ Listen, all the people have something important to tell you. Listening makes you learn from the people who are speaking (although you should also know when and how to cut the conversation when it goes to undesirable directions) and if in the talk you have the way to help the other person, you have already made your day ... You learned and helped at the same time.

+ Be honest and strong in your values, people in companies and in business (and in personal life), look for who gives them confidence, not necessarily for the most prepared one. We all prefer Honesty and values in the people that surround us and with whom we associate.

Honesty is an expensive value, do not expect it from cheap people.

+ Don't do to others what you wouldn't want them to do to you.

+ If you do not have something good to say about someone, you better not say anything.

+ Punctuality, respect your time and the others time.

+ Relate with successful people. If you have relationships with positive, enterprising people, with energy will help you to have a better attitude and your chances of success will be greater.

+ Not everything in life is work, you need to have a balance with exercise, food, health, fun and always look for the main thing that is the Family **and God.**

+ If you are going to do sales work, just do it if the other person really needs your product, it is not about making money, but that the money you make is helping others.

+ Read a lot, there are always things to learn, even from the topics that we know. If at any time you think you know everything about a topic ... we lost you Houston, Nobody knows everything about a topic.

Preferably read topics that make you grow, not novels or other topics, which are not bad, but the best reading is the one where you can learn something.

+ Learn another language, every time there are more foreigners working in all countries (which was previously rare) and internet commerce multiply the possibilities of making relationships / business with people from other countries.

+ Eat healthily and exercise, God gave you a body that you should take care of.

+ Do not be afraid of failure ... failure is necessary to succeed. In some groups of successful people, they measure how many failures they had to know how successful they are going to be. If you didn't had several failures, you are not consider with enough experience to make a successful business. Obviously you must learn from each failure and not be wrong in the same things, because there are also people who have broken several businesses, but always making the same mistakes.

We should have criteria because it is also true the saying, that there is nothing more dangerous than an idiot with initiative, the first time I heard this I laughed a lot, but seeing the things that people do business, it's scary.

+ Never suppose, fortunately we are not in a soap opera in which problems are generated because the protagonist thinks that the woman of his dreams does not want him and vice versa ... if you have any doubt, ask him / her, communication is very important and everything must be clear.

The same way in the school or courses, if you have doubt, you need to ask. Unfortunately we live in a society that sees the one who asks the question as the dumb ... and many times we prefer not to ask so the other people don't think that we are dumb. The truth is that we all have at least a couple of doubts in each class and the bad thing is that if everyone asks their questions, the class will not advance in the topics. Take advantage of the fact that others do not ask so you can make your questions and be the one who gets the most out of the class.

I hope that these tips and the rest of the book will help you in your personal and professional life, since this is the objective of this book ... to help you grow.

BIBLIOGRAPHY

* Images of search engines as Freepik, Storyblocks y Unplash.

ABOUT THE AUTHOR

CARLOS RAMOS

CPA with a Master's Degree in Finance, graduated from ITESM Campus Monterrey, with more than 20 years of experience in the Finance area (Finance Director, Controller, Accounting Manager) in both Public and Private companies. In sectors such as Automobile, Manufacturing, Ceramics, Mining and Services. With international experience, leading companies from Detroit Michigan and Salt Lake City, Utah.

Consultant in the Firm CPRQ Consultoría.

Webinar of How to identify losses to increase profits.

Participation in RCG Television programs of Business Finances and Personal Finances.